~WHERE'S THE~ WITCH?

First published in Great Britain in 2019 by Buster Books,
an imprint of Michael O'Mara Books Limited,
9 Lion Yard, Tremadoc Road, London SW4 7NQ

 www.mombooks.com/buster   f Buster Books   𝕏 @BusterBooks

This book contains material previously
published in *Where's the Penguin?*

A CIP catalogue record for this book is available from the British Library.

ISBN: 978-1-78055-645-1

1 3 5 7 9 10 8 6 4 2

This book was printed in August 2019 by
Shenzhen Wing King Tong Paper Products Co. Ltd.,
Shenzhen, Guangdong, China.

WHERE'S THE WITCH?

Buster Books

ILLUSTRATED BY
CHUCK WHELON

WRITTEN BY GARY PANTON

DESIGNED BY JOHN BIGWOOD AND JACK CLUCAS

A Trick-or-Treat Trip!

Halloween is just around the corner, and for Wendy the Witch
and her friends that can only mean one thing – trick-or-treating!
This year, to make it extra special, Wendy is taking the gang to
her favourite trick-or-treating locations all over the world.

It's going to be the trip of a lifetime – but they're also on
a tight schedule, because they need to get back home to
their haunted house in time for the big Halloween party.
Can you help Wendy by keeping a close eye on everyone?

Make sure you spot all ten of the creepy crew in each place.
When you're done, check your answers at the back
of the book and take a look at the Spotter's
Checklists for more fun things to find.

Wendy

When she's not zooming around on her broomstick and cackling, Wendy likes to read scary stories to her pet cat, Ian.

Mumford

Travelling the world is a big step for Mumford. He may look scary, but he's very shy and likes to keep himself under wraps.

Zoe

Zoe is a big fan of the great outdoors and is especially fond of shuffling around graveyards while wailing.

Frankie

Frankie is a monster with a big heart (which he sometimes shows to his friends at parties).

Bones

Bones is the group's champion breakdancer. No one can spin on their head faster than this guy.

Vera

Vera the Vampire is always getting up to mischief. She loves to play frightful pranks on the rest of the gang.

Pumpkin Pete

Pete started out as a regular scarecrow, but was brought to life by one of Wendy's spooky spells.

Gabby

Ghostly Gabby loves to make people jump. She's not happy unless she's floating through a wall and yelling 'BOO!'

Glurgle

Glurgle is a space slug from Planet Squelch who can't stop talking – but she only speaks Squelchese, so no one else understands her.

Wolfgang

Wolfgang is the group's party animal. Wherever he goes, he likes to make sure everyone has a howling good time.

Fancy Dress Party

The awesome thing about being a witch, vampire or enchanted scarecrow is that, when you go to a fancy dress party, you can turn up in your own clothes.

Wendy has brought the ghoulish gang to a huge outdoor dress-up bash, where Pumpkin Pete is living out his cowboy dream and Wolfgang is catching up with an old friend. Now hunt down all the others.

Fun in the Sun

Next up is a trip to the lake, where people have come from all around to splash in the water and enjoy the sunshine. It's very busy here, but the bone-chilling bunch are sure they'll fit right in.

Bones is playing with a friendly dog, while Wolfgang enjoys an ice cream (or, as he calls it, an ice SCREAM!). Can you spot what all the others are doing?

Animal Antics

Everyone loves a trip to the zoo.
The animals at this one are used to
being visited by girls and boys, but less
used to seeing a trick-or-treating witch,
ghastly ghost and squelchy space slug.

While Bones gets some exercise,
Zoe is making a new friend. It seems
everyone is causing mischief. Can
you find them all, before they
get into any more trouble?

PENGUIN SPOTTER TOURS

Snow Problem

Antarctica is very cold, and most of the locals are penguins. Mumford is all wrapped up so he's not too worried, but Bones is convinced he's got frostbite.

Zoe is practising her photography skills, while Vera tries to put her off. What are the others doing down here at the bottom of the world?

Market Mayhem

The frightful friends have found the perfect spot for trick-or-treating. This busy market is full of great bargains, but the blazing sun is a bit much for some of the gang.

While Mumford takes a dip to cool off, Glurgle is gurgling down a refreshing drink. Can you find the rest of the group?

Ocean Adventures

The deepest ocean is no ordinary place to go trick-or-treating – but these are no ordinary trick-or-treaters. If that shipwreck on the seabed wasn't haunted before, it sure is now.

Wendy has decided this is the perfect opportunity to try out her broomstick's underwater upgrade. Can you find her and her pals?

Slide and Swim

This water park is wet and wild! Everyone here is having so much fun that they probably won't even notice if the petrifying pals sneak in for some trick-or-treating … will they?

While Wolfgang keeps an eye on everyone, Bones gets back into the spirit of his good old days as a pirate captain. Shiver me timbers! Can you spot the others as well?

A Grand Feast

All of this travelling around has made everyone peckish. So, it's off to this fancy restaurant for a high-class evening of the best food money can buy. Let's hope no one misbehaves ...

Zoe is a bit disappointed that there are no brains on the menu, but everyone else is excited to have a fabulous feast. Can you see all ten of them?

The Big Concert

Wendy thinks classical music is fang-tastic. She usually listens to it through her earphones while flying around town on her broomstick, so to come to a live performance is a real treat.

It turns out Zoe, Bones and Frankie have some hidden talents and can't resist getting involved. But what are the others doing?

Carnival Capers

It's nearly time to head back home for the Halloween party, but first Wendy has one more treat in store for her friends – a huge carnival! There's music, dancing and so many masks that it's hard to tell the people from the monsters.

While Gabby shows off her musical skills, Vera is proving she really knows how to get ahead of the crowd. Where is everyone else?

Home Sweet Home

Hooray! The gang has made it home in time for the big Halloween bash. Friends and family have travelled from far and wide to be here, and some have even come back from the dead to celebrate their favourite day of the year.

While Wendy's witchy friends help her come in for a smooth landing, Pumpkin Pete is sharing travel stories with his family. Can you find the whole gang one last time?

Answers

Spotter's Checklist

- Someone dressed as a ladybird ☐
- A girl playing with bubbles ☐
- A girl dressed as a cheerleader ☐
- A plate of cupcakes ☐
- Someone dressed as a mermaid ☐
- A dog stealing sausages ☐
- Someone dressed as a giraffe ☐
- A girl being given a present ☐
- Someone dressed as a pig ☐
- A birthday cake ☐

Fancy Dress Party

Fun in the Sun

Spotter's Checklist

A man playing the guitar

A pink football

A mermaid

A girl doing a handstand

A red kayak

A red, yellow and green flag

A boy picking up some seaweed

A man using binoculars

A boat with blue sails

A girl with pink hair

Animal Antics

Spotter's Checklist

A boy wearing an elephant mask	☐
A yellow bug	☐
A monkey reading a newspaper	☐
A penguin wearing a bow tie	☐
An owl	☐
A boy slipping on a banana skin	☐
A scared snake	☐
A bucket of fish	☐
A broken fence	☐
A cheeky raccoon	☐

Spotter's Checklist

irate penguin	☐
olourful beach ball	☐
enguin with binoculars	☐
aby seal	☐
enguin with a guitar	☐
obot	☐
enguin reading a book	☐
green and yellow hat	☐
enguin superhero	☐
nap	☐

Snow Problem

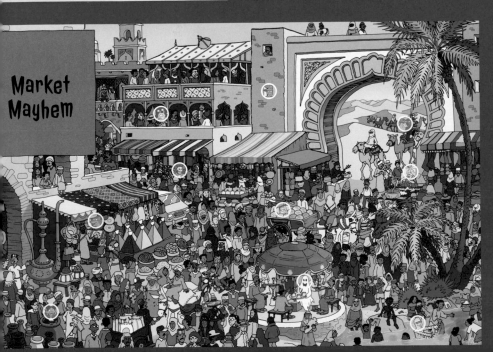

Market Mayhem

Spotter's Checklist

Someone falling off a camel	☐
A satellite dish	☐
A tourist with a video camera	☐
A man riding a donkey	☐
A mum and child on a motorbike	☐
An old man with a walking stick	☐
A man in a blue baseball cap	☐
A waiter pouring tea	☐
A woman with a purple bag	☐
A man sitting on a window ledge	☐

Ocean Adventures

Spotter's Checklist

An anchor

A whale

A treasure chest

A sea snail

A castaway

A pelican

Three seahorses

Two turtles

An orange, blue and white fish

A sword

Spotter's Checklist

A man with spotty shorts

A pink elephant

A woman in a stripy bikini

A lifeguard pointing

A woman with a baby

A man drying his hair

A red bag

A boy in a snorkel and mask

Someone with green hair

A girl being hit by a water gun

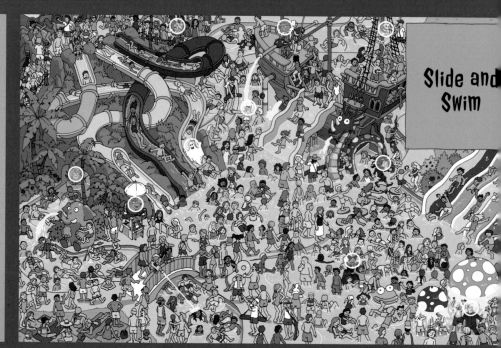

Slide and Swim

A Grand Feast

Spotter's Checklist

A robot waiter

A tall stack of plates

A bald man with a pink bow tie

A man looking at his watch

A chef in a pink uniform

A penguin-shaped ice sculpture

A man going to the bathroom

A boy sticking his tongue out

A giant green cocktail

A cheeseboard

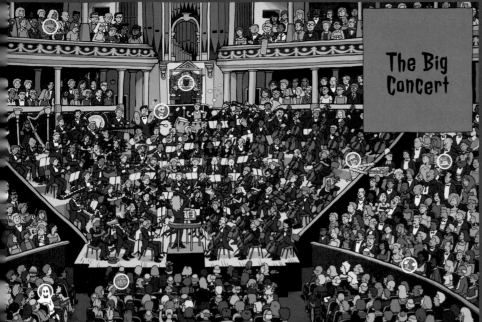

The Big Concert

Spotter's Checklist

- A pizza delivery guy
- A man with his fingers in his ears
- A musician wearing a sombrero
- A woman knitting
- A girl reading a book
- A musician blowing bubbles
- A man with a video camera
- A man eating popcorn
- A baseball cap with a propeller
- A musician in blue dungarees

Spotter's Checklist

- [Tw]o people dressed as chickens
- [A m]an in a pirate costume
- [A w]izard with a long beard
- [A g]iant alligator
- [A m]an in leopard-print pants
- [Th]e sun and the moon
- [Som]eone in a butterfly mask
- [A c]ouple in skeleton masks
- [A m]an wearing a monocle
- [A c]lown wearing a yellow hat

Carnival Capers

Home Sweet Home

Spotter's Checklist

- A toad with pink eyes
- A vulture with a rat in its beak
- A UFO
- A mad scientist
- A vampire child
- A knight in armour
- A maid with a feather duster
- A trio of hairy monsters
- A picture in a frame
- A vampire with yellow eyes